D0518675

JANE AUSTEN'S
ENGLAND

JOHN CURTIS

Text by Richard Ashby

SALMON

INTRODUCTION

Jane Austen was born in 1775 in the rectory at Steventon, a Hampshire village near Basingstoke, and lived here for the first twenty five years of her life. After three years in Bath and a number of temporary homes she returned to Hampshire with her mother and sister and the last eight years of her life were spent at Chawton, just twenty miles from her birthplace. Jane led a life typical of the daughters of the clergy, landed gentry and the minor aristocracy who people her novels. However, she was unusual in becoming a writer, at a time when most lady-like pursuits did not extend beyond a little needlework, sketching and piano playing. She and her sister were country lovers and great walkers. Although we associate her with the elegance of Bath there is no doubt that she was happiest in the country; and it is the villages, rectories and great houses that provide the backdrop to her characters. She wrote about what she knew; her kind of society, their entertainments and excursions, the country in which she lived and the houses that she visited. Jane Austen's country is largely the south of England; she disliked London, she went no further north than Warwickshire and it is doubtful if she ever saw hills higher than the Cotswolds. Her England is seemingly untouched by the wars raging on the continent and the Industrial Revolution at home but within this small compass is a complete world of social life and manners which still has a universal appeal.

Steventon Church

STEVENTON

The church in which she was baptised and one farm are all that is left of the Hampshire village that Jane would have known. Her nephew, William Knight, became rector in 1823 and built a new rectory on a new site in the village and Jane's old home was pulled down. While much is changed, the road between the site of the old rectory and the church, which Jane often walked, must be much the same.

READING ABBEY

It would have been very expensive to educate his five sons at boarding school so, unusually, Mr Austen educated them at home along with the sons of old university friends as classmates. It was the girls, Cassandra and Jane, who were sent away to school. At the early age of seven they attended a school, established by a relative, in Oxford which then moved to Southampton for a few months. Here Jane caught a fever and had to be quickly taken home again. Later, when Jane was ten, the sisters attended a boarding school for young ladies in Reading run by a Mrs La Tournelle who was renowned for her wooden leg made out of cork. The school occupied the imposing gatehouse which was the only substantial remains of the 12th century Reading Abbey.

ABBOTS WALK

GOODNESTONE PARK

Jane often stayed with her brother Edward and his wife Elizabeth at their house in Rowling, a few miles from Canterbury. She would often visit Elizabeth's parents at Goodnestone nearby to dine, to dance and to meet the varied company at the balls which play such an important part in her novels.

HURSTBOURNE TARRANT

Visits to friends or relations often lasted quite a long time. At the age of seventeen Jane stayed with Mary and Martha Lloyd at Ibthorpe and walked the rolling Hampshire countryside around the hamlet and the nearby village of Hurstbourne Tarrant. She described herself and Martha as 'desperate walkers'.

THE PARAGON, BATH

The Austen family had connections with Bath stretching back a good many years. Jane's parents were married in Walcot parish church, close to the house in The Paragon which was owned by Mrs Austen's brother. Jane and her family had stayed here on their first visit to Bath in 1797 and it was their temporary home while they went looking for a house when they first moved to the city in 1801. It faces the London Road which even then must have been very busy with traffic, but the rear looks out over the River Avon to the countryside and hills beyond.

CANTERBURY

Canterbury, dominated by its magnificent cathedral, would have been the object of shopping expeditions when Jane was staying at Rowling with her brother Edward. His adoptive mother, Mrs Knight, had a town house in the city and settled there after her husband died. She was very fond of Jane.

GODMERSHAM CHURCH

Edward had been adopted by childless, distant relatives, the Knights, and inherited Godmersham Park. Jane enjoyed her visits to Kent; it was 'the only place for happiness' she said. The family worshipped in the church of St Lawrence the Martyr which still contains a memorial to Edward's adoptive parents.

BOX HILL

Jane had cousins at Great Bookham. She would call on them on her way to Kent and stayed with them several times so would have been familiar with the surrounding countryside. She undoubtedly visited the Surrey beauty spot of Box Hill, the destination of the famous excursion in *Emma*.

LYME REGIS

It was a new interest in nature along with better roads and, indeed, boredom with the artificial life of spas like Bath, that led to the development of the seaside holiday. Resorts like Sidmouth, Weymouth and, most famously of all, Brighton vied with each other to attract the wealthy and genteel to the delights of sea bathing and healthy air. Jane's last unfinished novel *Sanditon* records the development of such a place. Jane and her family were early pioneers and one of their holidays was to the Dorset seaside village of Lyme which was just beginning to develop into the charming Regency town we know today. The spectacular breakwater, 'The Cobb' which remains such a prominent feature of the sea front, was begun in medieval times to shelter the little harbour from the open sea and the prevailing south-westerly winds. Jane and her family would undoubtedly have walked here and it is from the treacherous steps on the inner wall, the so-called 'Granny's Teeth', that Louisa Musgrove throws herself into the arms of the startled Captain Wentworth in *Persuasion*.

SYDNEY GARDENS, BATH

The decision of her father to retire to Bath came as quite a shock to Jane who dreaded leaving the quiet of the country. It is said that he fainted on hearing the news. It took quite a search, before the Austens settled on a house just opposite Sydney Gardens, with open country not far away and level access to the city's attractions along nearby Pulteney Street. The pleasure gardens had been laid out in 1795, only a few years before the Austens came to the city and it was, and remains a lovely place to stroll. Public breakfasts, concerts and fireworks added to its attractions. Jane was sent by her mother to find a husband here! She didn't succeed!

THE ASSEMBLY ROOMS, BATH

The large and modern Assembly Rooms in the upper part of the town were where Jane and many of her characters came to dance. However, by the time she came to live here, Bath was losing its popularity as the wealthy and the fashionable moved away from the city to the new seaside resorts and the Assembly Rooms were not as well-patronised as they had been when Jane was younger.

THE PUMP ROOM, BATH

Part of the 'cure' at Bath was to 'take the waters' regularly and the beautiful, elegant Pump Room overlooks the King's Bath. The fashionable assembled twice a day to drink a glass, pumped from the spring below and to see and be seen. The Pump Room was also a meeting place and a book was kept in which new arrivals were required to write their names and addresses so that everyone could see who was in town!

BLAISE CASTLE, BRISTOL

Jane had visited Bristol while at Bath and lived in Clifton for a short time after the family had left Bath. Rich Bristol merchants were building grander houses for themselves outside the city and the Blaise estate with its grand house, and grounds landscaped by Humphrey Repton was one of these. The 'castle' was a Georgian folly. In *Northanger Abbey*, John Thorpe tempts a reluctant and naïve Catherine Moorland with a trip from Bath to see these ruins, 'the oldest in the kingdom' with dozens of towers and long galleries, 'the finest place in England'. It is a joke, of course, the folly was barely 30 years old when Jane made her first visits to Bath.

STONELEIGH ABBEY

Originally a Cistercian Abbey dating from the twelfth century, Stoneleigh, in Warwickshire, had come into the hands of the ancestors of Jane's mother, the Leigh family, who had built an Elizabethan house in the ruins. Subsequently a great Classical front had been added, hiding the older parts of the house. Jane visited here with her mother in 1806 and they found everything very fine and beautiful but also very grand; Mrs Austen proposed that "directing posts at the angles" be set up to help people find their way around the enormous building. Stoneleigh is thought to be the original model for Sotherton in *Mansfield Park*. Jane describes Fanny Price's visit to the chapel, with its mahogany box pews and ornate plasterwork; "a spacious, oblong room, fitted up for the purpose of devotion".

THE CITY WALLS, SOUTHAMPTON

A year or so after the death of Jane's father she left Bath with her mother and sister and came to live in Southampton. She had been at school there and had visited it and danced there while living at Steventon so she already knew it well. Their house was just above the city walls, its probable site now occupied by a half-timbered pub.

THE DOLPHIN HOTEL, SOUTHAMPTON

Jane liked Southampton; it had the advantage of being in her own home county and on the sea. It was also a spa and had pretensions of becoming a resort. All the facilities which were required by fashionable society were provided; a Pump Room, Baths and two Assembly Rooms, one of them at The Dolphin Hotel, which still survives.

PORTSMOUTH

Two of Jane's brothers were in the Royal Navy and did very well in their chosen careers. Both brothers were based in this important naval base whose fortifications date from the Middle Ages. In *Mansfield Park* Fanny Price walks on these historic ramparts when she returns to Portsmouth, after a long absence, to see her family.

JANE AUSTEN'S HOUSE, CHAWTON

The bailiff's cottage at Chawton, owned by her brother Edward Knight, became Jane's home for the last years of her life. Probably Elizabethan in origin, it had been an inn, and later on was divided into three labourers' cottages. Now, one house again, it is the home of the Jane Austen Memorial Trust.

THE OLD BAKEHOUSE, CHAWTON

Jane Austen lived at Chawton for seven and a half years until her death in 1817. It was a very comfortable home with all the facilities that were considered necessary. At the back of the house the outbuildings included a granary and a bakehouse with an oven and a washtub. Nearby was a paddock for the donkeys which drew the carriage used by Jane when she became ill. It is still here.

JANE AUSTEN'S HOUSE, CHAWTON

Jane's brother made all the arrangements and so Jane and her family did not see the house before they moved in. Nevertheless, they were sure they would like it and were very happy here. Mrs Austen was a keen gardener, often helped by Cassandra. Jane and all the family enjoyed their garden at Chawton, indeed, Jane was enquiring about the kitchen garden before they moved in! The garden was larger than today with an orchard and a vegetable garden as well as flower beds and a shrubbery, and they also kept chickens. Together they planned their improvements to give them privacy from the road and places to walk.

THE DINING PARLOUR, CHAWTON

Now that Jane had a settled home, at last she could take up her writing again and the years at Chawton were very productive. *Sense and Sensibility* and *Pride and Prejudice* were revised and then published while she lived here, and three novels, *Mansfield Park*, *Emma* and *Persuasion* were written here. Her day always started with music. She practised the piano before breakfast, at which she presided, and then stayed in the dining parlour to write at a little table near the window which looked out on to the main roads where she could see the activities of the village and the passing of the stage-coaches.

OLD COTTAGES, CHAWTON

Jane's brother Edward also inherited Chawton Great House which was just a few minutes walk from Chawton Cottage. There would undoubtedly have been much coming and going between the two houses through the village and past these old cottages which have remained largely unchanged over two centuries.

CHAWTON GREAT HOUSE

The return to this part of Hampshire meant that the family could be closer together again. Steventon was not too far away and just a stroll away, through the village, was her brother Edward's Chawton Great House.
He spent part of each year here with his eleven children. It became the home of Jane's brother Frank and his wife Mary, and their sixth child was the first to be born in the Elizabethan house for over a hundred years. There were many visitors and Jane's other brothers often stayed here too. In view of its close association with Jane Austen it is appropriate that Chawton Great House is now a centre for the study of early English women's writing.

CHAWTON CHURCHYARD

Jane's mother died in 1827 and her sister in 1845. They are buried next to each other in Chawton churchyard. To many it must seem a shame that Jane, who was so close in life to her mother and sister and from whom she was never separated for long, should be buried by herself in Winchester Cathedral. The church at Chawton, dedicated to St. Nicholas, stands in idyllic surroundings beside the drive to Chawton Great House.

COLLEGE STREET, WINCHESTER

The cathedral city of Hampshire is only some 15 miles away from both Steventon and Chawton so Jane Austen certainly knew it from her visits. In 1816 her health began to give cause for concern, although in the periods of remission she found the strength to start *Sanditon*. She was under the care of a doctor from the County Hospital in Winchester. In order to be nearer to him she and Cassandra came to stay in the city in May 1817. They lived in a little house near to the gate into Winchester College and opposite the walls around the cathedral close. There was no cure for her illness and she died here in the arms of her sister two months later.

WINCHESTER CATHEDRAL

There were family connections with the cathedral and, as a resident of the parish of St Swithun, Jane was entitled to be buried there. In those days it was the custom that funerals were only attended by the men of the family. Cassandra, with whom Jane had spent so much of her life, watched from the upstairs window in College Street as the cortège made its way to Jane's last resting place in the cathedral's north aisle.

JANE AUSTEN MEMORIAL, WINCHESTER

When she died, Jane was practically unknown as an author outside her family circle. The only acknowledgement of her writing on the gravestone is to 'the extraordinary endowment of her mind'. But as her fame and reputation grew her nephew wrote the first complete biography and from the proceeds paid for the brass plaque which is on the wall nearby.

Published in Great Britain by J. Salmon Ltd., Sevenoaks, Kent TN13 1BB. Telephone 01732 452381. Email enquiries@jsalmon.co.uk
Design by John Curtis. Text and photographs © John Curtis (except photograph on page 16 © John Curtis/Bath & North East Somerset Council). All rights reserved.

ISBN 1-902842-65-0   Printed in Italy © 2005

Title page photograph: Sydney Place, Bath, Somerset
Front cover photograph: Jane Austen's House, Chawton, Hampshire
Back cover photograph: Gay St. from the Circus, Bath, Somerset